A Warrior
Blends with Life

A Modern Tao

A Warrior
Blends with Life

A Modern Tao

Michael A. LaTorra

North Atlantic Books
Berkeley, California

Published by
North Atlantic Books
P.O. Box 12327
Berkeley, California 94701

Cover and book design by Paula Morrison
Typeset by Catherine Campaigne
Printed in the United States of America

A Warrior Blends with Life: A Modern Tao is sponsored by the Society for the Study of Native Arts and Sciences, a nonprofit educational corporation whose goals are to develop an educational and crosscultural perspective linking various scientific, social, and artistic fields; to nurture a holistic view of arts, sciences, humanities, and healing; and to publish and distribute literature on the relationship of mind, body, and nature.

Library of Congress Cataloging-in-Publication Data

LaTorra, Michael, 1953–
    A warrior blends with life : a modern Tao / Michael LaTorra.
      p.   cm.
    ISBN 1–55643–160–0
    1. Lao-tzu   Tao te ching.   I. Lao-tzu   Tao te ching   English
1993.   II. Title.
BL1900.L35L388   1993
299'.51482—dc20   93–12491
                                        CIP

2 3 4 5 6 7 8 9 / 97 96 95

For the Giver of Life —

Table of Contents

Preface

Life is war by other means because war is the ultimate form of competition, where the stakes are life and death. In the game of life, the stakes are the same. But more is involved than competition. Cooperation is also necessary, whether in an army, cultural institution, business, marriage, or family. Still, competition persists everywhere in nature and culture, from swamp to city and beyond. Is that all there is?

Peace, like cooperation, is both possible and necessary. But competition is also an evolutionary, economic, and cultural necessity. So peace cannot be static, and therefore inimical to all forms of competition, or it stultifies and diminishes humanity. Real peace is dynamic, not dogmatic. It includes both free competition and voluntary cooperation.

Both are found in my free rendering of, and commentaries on, Lao Tzu's *Tao Te Ching*. Read this book with heart open and mind clear. After finishing, open the book again at random. Synchronicity is the next level.

> — *M. A. L.*
> 1992

Prologue
The Story

He was tired. When he looked beyond the boundary of his domain in the Royal Archives of China, he saw corruption and violence, repression and war. Lao Tzu decided to leave.

Lao Tzu did not leave with disgust; he left with compassion. He did not leave quickly by boat or horse. Lao Tzu went slowly by riding an ox, the better to meet people along his path.

But few people had time for Lao Tzu. Their daily lives were consumed in dealing with catastrophes of nature and man. Some watched the strange man on the ox, often catching something profound in his glance. But few spoke to him until he reached the final guard post on the western border of the kingdom at Han Gu Pass. The lone guard there stopped him.

"Lao Tzu, I recognize you!" the guard exclaimed. "I studied in the Royal Archives before falling out of favor and being sent here. Please, do not leave without sharing your wisdom!"

Lao Tzu dismounted his ox. He asked the guard to bring him brush, ink and paper. Then he sat quietly. After a while, Lao Tzu began to write. Then he sat quietly again. Alternately writing and sitting quietly, Lao Tzu carried on throughout a day and night.

Finally, he rose. Lao Tzu had written a book of 81 poems titled the *Tao Te Ching* ("Book of the Way"). In silence, he handed each of the 81 poems to the guard, one at a time.

The guard bowed as he accepted each poem. He read each in silence. Lao Tzu observed the man's face as he read, watching his eyebrows. First the eyebrows knotted, then relaxed as understanding came.

After reading the last poem, the guard knelt before Lao Tzu with tears in his eyes. "Please master, do not leave!"

Lao Tzu smiled. "With understanding and faith such as yours, distance and time do not matter. I have given you the keys. Use them."

Climbing atop his ox, Lao Tzu rode off to the west. The guard watched man and ox disappear down the road. He sighed.

Turning to the book, he began to read it a second time. He felt as if Lao Tzu were with him again. The guard soon discovered that each time he read Lao Tzu's words, he understood more and more about himself, and about the universe. His wisdom and joy increased. "Lao Tzu was right," he thought, "space and time do not matter."

Wisdom transcends time and space. It appears in different shapes for each age and place.

Now you are the guard. The book is in your hands.

A Modern Guide
to the Ancient
Way of Peace

1

The name that can be spoken is not the eternal name.
Names and beings evolve.
Everything changes.
Unchanging is the domain
of the bright nameless and timeless One.
The One is invisible
when you stand before the triple gates:
the iron gate of the past,
the flaming gate of the present,
the night-sky gate of the future.
Feel your heart in this play
of birth,
and life,
and death.
Sooner or later,
when the playing is done,
follow the Light to the One.

1

The blissful experience of out-of-body travel toward a great Light is common to people near death and to spiritual practitioners. Spiritual practitioners are men and women who can conduct latent energy from the base of their spines to the top of their heads by engaging the conscious process of infinite awareness. Similarly, in the process of dying, life energy flees the body via the spinal line and the individual gains awareness of higher levels of being. What is happening in both cases, in death (or near-death) and in mystical ecstasy, is a profound inversion of attention, and a withdrawal from external perceptions.

But for people near death (people who are clinically dead for some minutes) the experience is more disorienting. Like spiritual practitioners, they experience lights, see beings from other realms, and gravitate (most of them) toward a benevolent Light from above. How high you rise after death depends on what you do now, and also on what you do during the death experience. If you only learn one thing in this life, let it be this: Follow the Light to the One.

2

All qualities exist only in relation to their opposites.
Recognize beauty,
and you soon meet ugliness around the corner.
Hail goodness,
and you soon meet the shadow of evil.
Consider mere existence,
and you soon wonder about non-existence.
Each implies the other,
and cannot dance without its partner.

Difficult and easy define the range of effort.
Long and short measure relative space.
High and low gaze crook-necked at each other.
Front and back embrace each other.
Before and after step in time.

Be wise and live openly with apparent duality,
and paradoxical unity.
Measure, study, learn, and use everything harmoniously.
But grasp, cling to, and identify with nothing absolutely.
See what emerges from dynamic chaos:
evolving life,
growing wealth,
expanding understanding.
Be wise and let all things come and go as they will.
Own possessions but do not be possessed by them.
Try for your dreams but have no expectations.
When your work is done, forget it.
Your real accomplishments will last forever.

2

Your real accomplishments will last forever because they are not made of matter. Your real accomplishments are the sum total of how you lived your life. That determines where your essence goes after death. So, by all means, be involved in the world. Accomplish as much as you can here. But when your work here is done, forget it. Your real accomplishments will last forever.

3

If someone is idolized,
others plot jealously to get the same treatment.
If economic activity is restricted,
inevitable scarcity spews thieves.
If natural desire is punished,
anger shoves peace from the heart.

Be wise and encourage mutual satisfaction among all people.
Help each to empty noise from the mind,
and satisfy needs in the body.
Harness every ambition to the stars,
and temper setbacks with strong resolve.
Strengthen each essence.

When people are free of scarcity, disrespect, and hostility
no regulation is needed to maintain the state.

3

To free people of scarcity, have free markets. To rid people of disrespect, practice civility. To end hostility, be fair. When all this has been done, a natural state of affairs is permitted to arise. Because this state is natural, it is self-regulating. To maintain this state, no State is needed.

4

The absolute truth of the universe seems impossible to know.
Yet the search for truth is vastly rich in benefits.
We see one vast universe in space and time,
but it is actually nestled like a pearl
in an immensely bigger space
filled with pearls.
The absolute truth of the universe of universes
is the essence of all,
origin and end,
of all.

Each pearl universe has no sharpness,
yet it erodes all edges
of the myriad things and beings within it.
The truth is the Way a universe works.
The closer you come to it,
the more your universe works for you.

What has no tangible shape,
yet can untangle any complexity?
What is not glaringly obvious,
yet links the physics of light and the biophysics of brains?
What understanding can make sense of everything
from beginning to end?
It seems completely impossible to answer.
Yet truth is unchanging
whether you know the details or not.
You are never outside it,
but it can seem to be outside you.

The origin of origins cannot be spoken.
Yet fulfillment comes anyway,
when you align toward truth
in any and every way.
You don't need to know all the details of your universe
to be right with it.

4

Science is the method for uncovering more and more facts about the universe we inhabit. Spirituality is the method for uncovering more and more hidden truth within human beings. Separated at birth, these two great cultural forces are converging in our era.

As spirituality and science approach intersection, we can begin to see the dim outlines of the civilization their union will create. A civilization of harmony, health, wealth, happiness, and wisdom, this is the enlightened social order of Positive Futures.

5

Any universe is a machine of death,
a proliferator of bodies,
that doesn't give a damn about you and me.
Recognize the competition for life
inside the universal machine.

Be wise and discover how the machine works.
Discover all natural laws,
and redirect the machine as you will.
Use it to fulfill needs and expand life
as much as possible.
Discover your essence,
and you expand beyond all limits.
You are not essentially bound by the machine.

Realize it,
and you can depart the machine,
slowly or quickly,
and emerge into the Divine Domain,
blissful centerpoint of truth.

5

In the natural universe, we are mere animals. What becomes of us, each and all, is not really important. But in the universe of universes, in absolute and most fundamental terms, we are something more. Unlike animals, we can contemplate the mystery of our existence and our identity. Logic fails when we try to answer the simple question "Who am I?" No matter how we answer, we're always something greater than we can name. We are at once highly evolved primates and apparently immaterial minds. Yet over a lifetime both our bodies and our minds change so much that we can't claim to be the same person now as we were at the start. Your unique identity lies elsewhere.

Your true identity is a unique essence that lies below, above, and beyond all those other aspects of your body and mind that can be known to others. This mysterious essence is the real "you" in the deepest sense. When you realize your essence, breaking through the random circumstances of your life to its spiritual core, then even your body and mind change in remarkably positive ways. At that point, the creation of marvels begins.

6

The properties of life are eternally part of this universe.
Physics and chemistry make it so.
The organization of life grows more complex,
while entropy grows elsewhere.
This marvel is the root myth
of the female birthing process,
and all human creativity.
It is the mysterious origin.
You can't put your finger on it,
but it's always there when you need it.

6

The history of life on Earth is the rags-to-riches story of the single-celled organism that multiplied, diversified into all plants and animals, and took over the planet. The true origin of that first cell is not the chemistry and physics that made it possible, because they are built into the laws of the universe. The true origin of the first cell is the One who permits the universe to exist. That is the unfailing Source.

When you are desperate and you pray to God, you are addressing the mysterious, original Source. And as Lao Tzu says, "You can't put your finger on it, but it's always there when you need it."

7

Life is ancient on this ancient Earth.
Why is this so?
Life exploits all growth opportunities
without self-consciousness.
Therefore, it can endure indefinitely.
Be wise:
Live unself-consciously.
Recognize the needs of others
as opportunities for fulfillment.
Serve the needs of others
and all your own needs will be fulfilled.
If you do not fall into dilemma
over the paradox of ego-identity,
your consciousness is absolute.

7

Self-consciousness is self-torture. Self-consciousness, which is obsessive self-concern and ego-fixation, is like contorting your body to watch yourself over your own shoulder. Not only is this impossible, but you suffer for even trying.

8

Success is like water.
Its benefits flow to everyone near it,
even without planning to.
It doesn't protest falling to the bottom,
knowing it will rise again.
It is the true spirit of life.

Successful people adapt to any environment.
Successful people turn their minds to understanding.
In dealing with others, they are kind.
They speak truthfully.
They bring order to their responsibilities.
They prize efficiency.
They know when to act on an opportunity.
Because they do not irritate others,
everyone treats them with sincere respect.

8

Water falls as rain, gathers into streams, lakes, and rivers, flows to the sea, and then evaporates to fall as rain again in natural cycle. Water does not plan to provide sustenance to plants and animals along the way. It does not plan to irrigate our fields and gardens, to slake our thirst, to give us places for boating and fishing and swimming. Yet these benefits flow naturally from water doing what it does.

When humans are as free to flow as water, they naturally create free markets. Then each person, buyer and seller, may benefit from filling the needs of the other.

When humans are as free to flow as water, they naturally encourage free speech. Information is exchanged, knowledge accumulates, new discoveries are made and communicated, new inventions created, to the ultimate benefit of all.

When humans are as free to flow as water, they naturally follow the traditional watercourses. This is how the wisdom of the past is conserved.

9

Ever increasing tension
leads to catastrophic failure.
Too fine an edge
wears away quickly.
Monumental wealth brings insecurity.
Ostentation invites trouble.
Therefore, accomplish wealth and fame,
but recognize that enough is enough.
This is the Way of real success.

9

Relax. Don't show off. Be great, but humble. That's real success!

10

Can you act with body and mind
in unison?
Can you release bodily tension
like a newborn baby?
Can you clear your mind
of false impressions?
Can you love your people
and govern your domain
without self-importance?
Can you be receptive to the pulse of life
like a woman giving birth?
Can you observe all,
near and far,
great and small,
without interfering?

Create things and give birth to children.
Nurture them, but do not possess them.
Instruct, but do not control.
This is real integrity.

10

When body and mind are harmonized, they act in concert. This is the unity of the integral person. No superfluous bodily tension. No babbling brain programs. Integrity.

11

Spokes converge on an empty center
to make a wheel.
Without an empty center
there is no room for an axle.

Mold a cup.
Its emptiness makes it useful.
Put doors and windows in a house.
Interior space gives it value.

The usefulness of what is
depends on what is not.

11

Emptiness can be as valuable as fullness. You cannot add to what is already full. When your room is packed from floor to ceiling, you cannot add another treasure to it. When your muscles are chronically tense, you tire easily but rest uneasily. To make space in your room for a new treasure, remove an old one. To make room in your life for relaxation, release the tensions in body and mind. Empty space and relaxation of tension reveal the value of nothing. Nothing matters. And nothing can be good for you.

12

The world of colors distracts the eye.
The world of sounds deafens the ear.
The world of flavors dulls the palate.
Single-minded pursuit of pleasure narrows the mind.

Cultivate your interior life
and all things become new again.

12

Pleasures of the senses become tiring after a while. Periods of intense pleasure are best followed by periods of recuperation, or even regenerative retreat from the world, just as a good night's sleep follows an active day.

To tap the source of refreshment, open up to what's inside you.

13

Fortune and misfortune are both stressful.
If you think only of yourself,
both can drive you mad.

Why are fortune and misfortune both stressful?
One is not spiritually superior to the other.
You can be as overwhelmed by good fortune
as by bad.

Why can thinking only of yourself drive you mad?
Ego is an illusion,
like the false infinity of opposing mirrors.
If you understand the illusion,
you are free to be truly infinite.
Then how can anything upset you?

The universe includes your body.
Your body is not separate from the universe.
Serve one and you serve both.
Only faithful servants can be given
responsibility for everything.

13

Allow the surface clutter of your conventional mind to be swept away by the natural rhythms of your brain. Your body relaxes naturally. Deep feelings are free to surface when superficial clutter has gone. The hidden mechanisms of the world become apparent. You become faithful. Then you understand why Lao Tzu and Jesus agree that only faithful servants can be given responsibility for everything.

14

We look for it but cannot see it,
so we call it invisible.
We listen for it but cannot hear it,
so we call it silent.
We reach for it but cannot touch it,
so we call it impalpable.

Each of these three is too subtle for description.
By intuition you can see it,
hear it,
and feel it.
Then the unseen,
unheard,
and untouched
are present as One.

Face it
and you cannot see its face.
Follow it
and you cannot see its back.
Look up and it is not blazing.
Look down and it is not dark.
It does not stand out.
When you try to clarify it,
it dissolves completely.

It has been called the formless Form
and the imageless Image.
But the subtle One owns no name.

It is known by its effects.
Ageless and timeless,
you can ride it today forever.
Stay with it,
and you can manage whatever comes.
This is the essential Way.

14
———

At the beginning, spiritual life is a kind of letting go. But once the spirit is quickened, the process becomes a kind of holding on. Spiritual consciousness is an exhilarating ride to a most wonderful Destination.

15

In ages past and to come
the best of men and women
are subtle,
profound,
and receptive.
Their depths are unfathomable.
We can only describe their behavior.

Their actions are deliberate and unhurried,
as if crossing an icy stream in winter.
They seem cautious,
as if unsure of the people around them.
Their demeanor is reverent,
as if meeting honored guests.
They are not assertive,
as if strangers in an unknown land.
They are adaptable,
as ice turning to water.

They are simple and genuine,
like solid oak.
They are empty and receptive,
like a virgin valley.
Thorough and unbiased,
they treat all equally,
like a flooding river flowing to the sea.

Who but ones such as these
can start at the bottom

and end at the top?
Can you remain still
and so recharge your vitality?
Those who live this Way
do not try to fill themselves
to overflowing.
Because they are not overfull,
they are constantly renewed.

15

Lao Tzu describes the behavior of the mysterious sages as cautious, unhurried, reverent, unassertive, and adaptable. He says they are genuine, receptive, and unbiased. The sages do not fill themselves, so they always have room for more. Be like them.

16

Attain the complete clarity of emptiness.
Maintain perfect silence.

Amid the rush of worldly comings and goings,
observe how endings become beginnings.
Every creature eventually returns to its origin.
What was before birth is again after death.
To return to the origin is to be at rest.
This is called "renewal."
To be renewed is to realize radiant wisdom.
To realize radiant wisdom is to be clear of obstructions.
If you do not realize radiant wisdom,
you walk blindly off a cliff.
Realizing radiant wisdom, you become tolerant.
Becoming tolerant, your orientation is positive.
Positive orientation is alignment with the Way.
Alignment with the Way yields eternal life.

Be aligned with the Way,
and the death of your body
will not be your death.

16

Lao Tzu emphasizes that "alignment with the Way yields eternal life," so that "the death of your body will not be your death." The implication here is that you may or may not survive death.

Your essence always survives death, but the rest of yourself may not. The destiny an essence tries to fulfill through reincarnation in life after life is to integrate more and more parts of the person with the essence. Then more of the person survives death. If you become an essentially integrated person, you come through the process of dying to emerge whole in a different world. But if, for example, a man is not integrated—if he ignored the still, small voice of his essence all his life, and if he bit the hands stretched out to help him—then his essence cannot redeem his character. That character dies. And eventually, if his essence cannot integrate a viable person after several lifetimes, the essence will be retracted by the Source.

17

The best leader works without being seen,
helping all but known by few.
The second best leader is loved and praised.
The bad leader is feared and hated.
The worst leader is despised and ignored.

When a leader trusts no one,
no one trusts him.

The best leader is tight-lipped;
he never speaks carelessly.
When his subtle work is completed, his duty done,
ordinary people say,
"We did it ourselves."

17

The best leader guides, he does not govern. He makes suggestions, and lets people act. The best leader is a man of few words. He works in the background. His objective is to make himself obsolete.

18

When people first abandoned the Way,
propriety and rectitude were created.
When cleverness and record-keeping appeared,
hypocrisy began.
When family peace and unity ended,
praise of family values started.
When disorder beset the country,
public servants declared their patriotism.

18

The decline of a civilization begins with abandonment of the Way. The renewal of a civilization begins with return to the Way. At this time, we are on the cusp of transition between the farthest abandonment of the Way and the beginning of return to the Way. When we return to the Way this time, though, we do so as a global civilization preparing for a glorious destiny on Earth and in space. The Way is billowing into a rainbow of Positive Futures.

19

Forget the difference between spirituality and science,
and people will benefit a hundredfold.
Forget propriety and rectitude,
and people will return to natural harmony.
Forget cleverness and record-keeping,
and people will not lie and cheat.

These negatives are artificial strictures,
too weak to bear a civilization.

So heed these positive words:
Be simple.
Accept the facts as they are.
Discover your true heart's desire.
Don't let the learned worry you with theories.
And so discover your ultimate freedom.

19

—————

A civilization cannot be built on negative strictures, endless lists of "Do Not"s. A positive impulse is needed. Lao Tzu advocates simplicity and discovering your true heart's desire. A civilization built on those two positive impulses is the civilization of Positive Futures.

Your heart's desire, your own Positive Future, is integral to this civilization. No learned theorist can tell you what it is. Only you can know it.

Learn from religion and science and your own observation of the simple facts of existence. Don't worry about social niceties when you examine yourself. Accept the facts as they are. Discover your true heart's desire, and you will find your destiny. Pay attention and you'll understand. Act on your understanding, and you help build the civilization of Positive Futures.

20

Is there really much difference between
"yes" and "no"?
Is there any absolute distinction between
actions called "good" and "evil"?
Should you always do what everyone else does?
What a joke!

Other people are all smiles,
as if their lives are one big party.
I alone sit quietly
without a glimmer of merriment,
like a newborn saying nothing.
I move aimlessly or sit,
no goal in mind.

Other people make and spend fortunes.
They are smart and savvy.
I alone seem foolish,
earning little, spending less.

Other people strive for fame.
I avoid the limelight,
preferring to be left alone.
Indeed, I seem like an idiot!
No mind, no worries.

Other people are animated and confident.
I alone seem dull and unmotivated.
Like the ocean, I change unpredictably.

Other people are useful.
I alone am unexploitable.
But what really makes me so different
from other people?
I value only what comes from the Great Mother.

20

In the spiritual traditions, blissful states are associated with the female aspect of the One. Lao Tzu calls her the Great Mother. He describes the state of the Enlightened sage with emphasis on the sage's freedom from worldly striving. What is implied in the words "no mind, no worries" is a state of consciousness ultimately simple, profound, and blissful. It is the pearl of great price. The mind is clear even as the heart swoons with delight. No one in that state would trade it for the world.

21

One who is successful follows the Way.
Descriptions of the Way are chaotic and uncertain.
The Way itself seems chaotic and uncertain,
yet within it are patterns and entities.
Chaotic and uncertain,
yet within it is subtle essence.
Shadowy and indiscernible,
yet its power is immeasurable.
The power of this essence is subtle
but utterly real.
It is the root origin of all creation.
From the beginning
to the present
and into the future,
it is and was and will be.
Only its name has changed.
Through sincere commitment,
you may become one with it.

How do I know what it is like?
I look inside myself and see.

21

The essence is eternal. It is without beginning or end. Would you like to be eternal? "By sincere commitment, you may become one with it." To find out what it is like, look inside yourself and *see*.

22

The flexible are preserved unbroken.
The bent become straightened.
The empty are filled.
The exhausted become renewed.
The poor are enriched.
The rich are confounded.

This is why the successful
cling to nothing but the Way,
influencing others by their example.
Because they do not make spectacles of themselves,
everyone wants to bask in their light.
Because they are not pushy,
everyone wants to embrace them.
Because they do not boast of their accomplishments,
their success is guaranteed.
Because they do not strive for prominence,
no one can top them.

The old saying that the flexible are preserved unbroken
is surely right!
Truly, they will be preserved in the Way.

22

Flexibility is the ability to bend without breaking. If you can bend under the blows of chaotic life and always rise again, others will be encouraged by your example. People will be attracted to you, wanting to bask in your presence. Without boasting, you will find that your success becomes famous.

23

Incessant talking is against nature.

A tornado does not last all day.
A torrential rain does not last all week.
If nature's utterances cannot persist for long,
how much less can a human being's?

Those who follow the Way
become one with the Way.
Those who follow goodness
become one with goodness.
Those who stray from the Way and goodness
become one with failure.

If you conform to the Way
its power flows through you.
If you conform to goodness
goodness blesses you.
If you deviate from the Way and goodness
deviations surround and confound you.

Distrust others, and they will find
nothing to trust in you.

23

Stop gabbing. Consider how you can follow the Way, how to conform your life to goodness. Answers come quickly. So do blessings. Trust.

24

If you stand on tip-toe, you cannot stand firmly.
If you take long steps, you cannot walk far.
If you show off, you demean yourself.
If you insist you are always right, you are wrong.
If you boast of your prowess, you will fail.
If you take pride in yourself, you will not progress.

All of these are like unnatural hunger
for excessive food by the already obese.
Such things are rejected by most people.
So one who is successful passes them by.

24

The causes of failure are overreaching, exhaustion, showing-off, self-righteousness, boasting, and pride. Success comes from avoiding the causes of failure.

25

Before Heaven and Earth were created,
there was something formless yet complete.
Silent, untouchable, unitary, immutable.
It was self-sufficient, omnipresent, peerless.
You may think of it as the Mother of all things.
It is so far beyond humankind, it has no name.
As a nick-name, we call it the Way.
For lack of a better word, I call it "the Great."
Being great, it has no limits.
Having no limits, it reaches to infinity.
Reaching to infinity, it comes right back to itself,
the self-sufficient Origin.
In fact, it never really left!
This mysterious subtle energy
is truly the greatest of all.

The Great created the Way.
The Way created Heaven.
Heaven created Earth.
Earth created humanity.

Thus, to know humanity,
understand Earth.
To know Earth,
understand Heaven.
To know Heaven,
understand the Way.
To know the Way,
understand the Great within yourself.

25

The Way extends from the mysterious origin of the universe to the center of the human heart. "To know the Way, understand the Great within yourself."

26

Gravity is the root of levity.
Equanimity is the source of action.

Realizing this,
the successful person is
poised and centered
in the midst of all activities.
Though surrounded by opulence,
the successful person is not swayed.
It is dangerous for someone with grave responsibilities
to mistake sarcasm for humor.
In sarcasm your center is lost;
in humor it is restored.
Impulsive actions only lead to greater dangers!

26

    Only when you know the serious truth can you see the humor in it. Only when you can stay in place calmly are you ready to move.

27

Perfect action leaves no traces.
Perfect speech flows without flaw.
Perfect calculation needs no aids.
Perfect security seems unguarded,
but cannot be violated.
Perfect binding employs no rope,
but cannot be undone.

Be wise and help all beings impartially,
abandoning none.
Waste no opportunities.
This is called conducting the Light.
The wise person on the Way is the teacher of the ignorant.
The ignorant person off the Way is the student of the wise.
If the student does not value the teacher,
and the teacher does not attend to the student,
though both may be intelligent,
bewilderment reigns.

27

Perfection is the goal. Education is the means. Cooperation between student and teacher is the technique. Success in everything is the result.

28

Know in yourself the masculine principle,
but adhere to the feminine principle,
and so become like a valley
into which all things flow.
Being like such a valley,
you have a power that never fails.
This is called returning to the purity
of a newborn baby.

Know the light,
but adhere to the dark.
Never stray from truth,
and you become the measure of all things.
As the measure of all things,
you become one with the Infinite.

Know the extraordinary,
but adhere to the ordinary,
and so become like the universal valley.
Being like the universal valley,
your energy flow will always suffice.
In this manner, return to the unformed state.

When the unformed is formed into objects,
its original qualities are lost.
If you preserve your original qualities,
you can govern anything.
Truly, the best governor governs least.

28

The human body has two sides, just as the human species has two sexes. The two brain hemispheres are complementary, one offering linear logic, the other holistic pattern recognition. The brain hemispheres are cross-wired to the body: to feel the logic of the left brain, use the right side of your body; to feel the intuition of the right brain, use the left side of your body.

Balance is the key. People who achieve much and then boast about it are not secure in their accomplishments. People who achieve much and humbly thank those who helped them along the way are truly great.

Leaders claiming to help the people by creating huge service institutions only hurt the people by making them subservient to institutional bureaucrats. The best leaders help people by giving them the tools to help themselves.

29

Those who want to conquer the world never succeed.
World sovereignty has the subtle character
of a sacred chalice.
Tampering ruins it.
Grabbing it ruins the grabber.

Events cycle between alternatives.
Things move ahead, then fall back.
Attention focuses internally, then externally.
Growth comes, followed by decay.
One rises high, then sinks low.

Keep to the middle, avoiding all extremes,
in thought, feeling, and action.
If you do not cycle from pole to pole,
your equanimity lasts forever.

29

In this chaotic world of natural laws, biological accidents, and human competition, the shortest distance between your starting point and your goal is seldom a straight line.

What many people call "knowing who you are" is often only knowing who others want you to be and then acting that role. This can lead to hidden bitterness and despair. You may not feel that you really know who you are. Your role might feel confining, boring, or worse. Still, if you feel bound to fulfill your role, you want to do it happily. Why can't you? Because you don't really know who you are, in the deepest sense.

Paradoxically, the best way to fulfill your role and yourself is to realize your essential self, which is like no-self at all. Ego, personality, and being are composed of many parts, and the essence is just one small but absolutely necessary part. If you orient your life efforts toward increasing the influence of your essence among all the other parts of yourself, you grow more happy and more capable. The essence has no limits. Neither do you.

Cycles comprise the circuit of existence. For you and for everyone, there is a seeming beginning of existence at birth, a middle called life, and an ending called death. That is the situation of you, me, our species, our planet, our universe. But it's not the whole story. The whole story is circular. Each end is also a new beginning.

How does an end become a beginning? By what they have in common. Our cosmic situation of life and death is analogous to our daily experience of waking consciousness, dreaming sleep, and deep sleep. Each state of consciousness occurs in the same body. Whether you're walking down the street, or chasing rainbows in your dreams, or even being apparently unconscious in deep sleep, you are still you—you live. In the same way, your essence is still you no matter what experience you're having, in this body or out of it, after death. An end becomes a beginning because your essence is not limited by the events in the story—just as the dreamer is not killed by the dream. Once you realize this, you have greater freedom within the story to modify the outcome—to remain lucid in the dream. You become more capable of achieving your own Positive Futures.

30

One who advises a leader in the Way
counsels against conquest,
because today's conqueror
will be conquered in turn tomorrow.

Armies leave blight in their wake.
Sickness and scarcity follow war.

Therefore, a good general does only enough,
nothing more.
He never fights in his own name.
He fulfills his mission,
but is not vainglorious.
He fulfills his mission,
but does not boast.
He fulfills his mission,
but is not proud of violence.
He fulfills his mission,
only because he has no other choice.

Whatever strains with force,
will soon decay.
It is not attuned to the Way.
Not being attuned to the Way,
its end comes all too soon.

30

Apes fight over territory. So do humans. The wise avoid conflict if possible. But when conflict is inevitable because lives are threatened, the wisest course is to win. Not to win some vainglorious Pyrrhic victory, in which victor and vanquished are both radioactive ruins. Not to flatter the ego of ambitious leaders. But only this—to win. And to win only because you have no other choice.

31

Even fine weaponry is tarnished
by association with death and destruction.
They are avoided by followers of the Way.

According to ancient custom,
in peace the left-hand, receptive side
is the place of honor,
but in war the right-hand, active side
is the place of honor.

Weapons are not the tools of the wise.
They are used only as a last resort.
If weapons must be employed,
use them with deliberate restraint.

Wise people value peace most highly,
and refuse to decorate instruments of war.
Decoration shows admiration for death-dealers.
If you admire death-dealers,
you sign your own death warrant.

So on happy occasions,
give preeminence to the receptive left side.
On sad occasions,
to the assertive right.
The deputy commander stands on the left,
and the commander stands on the right,
to indicate the mournfulness of war.

Even in victory,
the dead of both sides must be remembered.

31
———

    After a war, a people must regain their balance. The right and left sides of the human body and brain function best when balanced. In society too, the active and receptive principles, used in war to build engines of death, switch in peace to building engines of creation. When this happens the final time, all humanity will be the victor.

32

The Way is eternal, but it is not a famous name.
If it could be compared to objects,
it would be the smallest and plainest,
yet nothing is superior to it.
If rulers would live it,
their subjects would be truly loyal
without coercion.
The social order and the natural order
would harmonize of their own accord.
When an assertive State awards distinctions,
envy arises.
When envy arises,
it is time to stop.
By stopping in time,
danger can be avoided.
Return to simplicity,
and harmony will be restored.

32

"The Way is eternal, but it is not a famous name." The Way is not a brand name. It simply *is*. It is the waterway coursing through the Great Being in which we live and breathe and move. Ride the flow and you can steer your life; fight against the flow and you get pulled under.

When you are in the balanced yet dynamic flow state, your life is like a nearly frictionless laminar current within the turbulent river of daily news. You maintain integrity amid chaos.

And flowing is fun. It's a ride. The first thrill you feel in a speeding vehicle, or on a surf board, or on a funway ride, is the thrill of acceleration. Acceleration is exhilaration. And exhilaration is a species of happiness just as valuable as its opposite, contemplative repose. Your body design contains physiological circuits of breath, blood, and nerves that need such positive stimuli to grow. But your essential consciousness is always already riding the circuit of reality. Go with the flow.

33

One who understands others has knowledge.
One who understands himself has wisdom.
One who overcomes others has force.
One who overcomes himself has true strength.
One who has contentment is rich.
One who forces the issue may win the day,
but he will lose in the end.
Only one who knows his own heart can endure.
When he dies, he does not perish.

33

Knowledge and wisdom are not the same. Observable facts are knowledge. Self-understanding is wisdom. A person can be well-educated, erudite, and clever, but stumble over his own feet because he does not understand how to tread his life's road. Another person, perhaps uneducated, might understand herself far better, and so live through her karmic lessons and get them over with more quickly. Meanwhile, the clever fool of sparkling wit cannot seem to get his life together.

After many years, death will come to both. She will look back on a full life, and then die with contentment, already intuiting her glorious destiny. His death will come suddenly, leaving little time to say all those dying words he wished so many to hear. So he will come back to this place again, like being left back a grade in school, reincarnated to learn the lessons he failed last term.

34

The creative energy of the Way is everywhere.
Up and down, left and right, in and out,
it flows without obstruction.
All creatures emerge because of it,
and it provides for them.
Even so, it does not take possession of them.
It accomplishes its purpose,
but makes no claims for itself.
It covers all creatures like the sky,
but does not dominate them.
Therefore, it is called Humble.
All creatures return to it,
and it contains them.
Therefore, it is called Great.
Be wise:
Do not make a show of greatness;
then you will be truly great.

34

Only a few of the truly great people have been famous. We all know the historically great spiritual teachers, the artists, scientists, and heroes. In addition, modern mass media foment mountain ranges of celebrities more extensive and varied than any pagan pantheon.

Unfortunately for the "immortal" celebrities of today, fame brings neither greatness nor eternal life. Far greater than the well-known are the many inconspicuous ones who bring life, love, and compassion to others face to face. These hidden saints are in every land. Everyone meets at least one each lifetime, even if just for a moment, and without recognition.

The kindness of strangers is no stranger than this.

35

Turn your attention to the imageless image of the Way,
and all is right with the world.
Your peace and freedom outshine the surroundings.
Speak your wisdom to others,
and they yawn.
"So obvious and ordinary!" they say.
The Way is not like exciting music and tasty food,
that any fool can appreciate.
The Way does not advertise itself like flowers to bees.
Never exhausted, eternally useful,
you must recognize it for what it is.

35

The secret protects itself.

36

If you want to grow outwardly, first grow inwardly.
If you want real strength, learn to yield.
If your ambition is only fame, humiliation follows.
If you cling unyieldingly to anything or anyone,
they will surely be taken away.
This is the subtle law of the universe:
Opposites exchange positions.

Be wise:
The soft and yielding can overcome the hard and strong.
The strength of a country or person is better hidden.
Fish cannot leave the deep,
and you cannot escape the consequences of the law.
Realize your essential nature beyond
identification, differentiation, and desire.
Wise acts inflict no consequences.

36

Opposites attract, in nature and in us. You are always tending to move toward balance by seeking your complementary opposite. Over time, you become like the object of your thoughts. Be careful what you wish for.

The law of love and life is this: What you meditate upon, you become. Cherish the highest love-wisdom, and your life will be unlimited.

37

The Way is never preoccupied,
yet nothing is left undone.

If leaders of the world sunk their roots in the Way,
world affairs would flow into natural coherence.

The solution to confusion is simplicity.

When life is simple,
pretenses fall away;
our essential natures shine through.

A peaceful social order liberates human energies.

37

Some people feel guilty if they're not worrying about doom, disaster, and the guilt of others. They crave causes to be self-righteous about. Their preoccupations are endless, and they know no peace beyond rhetoric. In this, they resemble greatly the leaders they wish to replace.

Simply work together for mutual satisfaction in free markets, and you can rely less on leaders. Be unpretentious and straightforward in speaking the truth, and you can reach understandings that achieve peace. Do this essential work, and you become the leader you wished to find.

38

A truly good person is not self-conscious about goodness.
No narcissism.
People striving to meet
every conventional rule about goodness
wear themselves out.

A truly good person is simply relating to all experiences
in full feeling of absolute being.
People striving for relative social merits
are always planning strategies to win.
They resort to hollow benevolence,
advertised righteousness,
and charm.
If that fails,
they take up weapons.

When people estrange themselves from the Way,
they can't see themselves as they are.
They hide their ignorance by pretending.
When pretense fails,
social contracts are written.
When social contracts fail,
teachers of salvation appear.
When the teachers are long dead,
organizations rule ceremoniously.
When only ceremony and etiquette are left,
people lack loyalty and kindness.
Their society enters the chaos
preceding the next cycle of history.

After people have been tested by life they value
truth,
the current of inner fulfillment,
the patience of high indifference,
and perfect timing.

38

We are at the cusp of a major cycle of history. Human civilization is growing more global every day, but change has come faster than societies can easily adapt. So the current civilization falls apart even as the new civilization is coming together.

For a number of years to come, the human family will creak along under the stress of transition. But soon a confluence of forces, ancient and new, will give us the tools and the time to rebuild our lives. Once the rough decades are over, we can live again at the ancient pace of life enjoyed in some lost golden age, supported not by human servants this time, but by mechanical mind children, machines that do our bidding without dilemma. Modern life-stress among our species will be reduced beneficially. Wisdom will have time to grow.

39

In every age,
some individuals realize their essential nature.
They become aware of who they are:
clear as a starry night sky,
singular as the Earth,
surrounded by beings in many realms,
above and below their own.

A rock can't stop being a rock.
It is part of the Way,
but it has no conscious destiny.
Human beings can seem to be very different.
They have free will to wander off the Way.
Then, eventually, they succumb to mere fate,
instead of their true destiny,
their highest Positive Future.

Be wise:
Serving others with love
magnifies your radiance.
Cultivating your essence with care
prolongs your enjoyment.

Wandering far from the Way
leads to declining quality
of life, health, and sanity.
Storms, earthquakes, and news of death
unnerve even the unthreatened.

The Way is open to you at any moment.
Real success comes by plain perseverance.
Only you can judge yourself.
Humility in greatness is essential.
The Way offers rewards beyond counting.
Accept them humbly.

39

You have free will. You may follow the Way, or not. That is your choice. The wise choose to serve the Way of radiant love and unlimited life. In every age, some few have realized It completely. In ages to come, more will have the opportunity than ever before. As humanity grows spiritually and materially, wealth permits more individuals the time to ask themselves the Buddha Questions:

Where did I come from?

Who am I?

Where am I going?

The Great Answer to all three questions is: the Infinite. You originate in the Infinite Source. Your essential being is the Infinite Presence. And your highest Positive Future is epochal growth up and beyond the heights of all universes to your transcendentally Infinite Home.

40

Going away
then coming home
is the exercise of the Way.
Gentle and yielding
is the Way in use.
Everything you can see
originated in what you can't see.
Follow the Way to the Source.

40

Go home.

41

When insightful people hear of the Way
they take it up immediately,
seeking unity.
When mediocre people hear of the Way,
they are unimpressed.
When people who are lost hear of the Way,
they laugh derisively.
If it were not laughed at,
it would not be true.

Since ancient times it has been said:
People who understand the Way seem simple.
Those who approach the Way seem ordinary.
People riding close to wave crests
in the current of the Way,
live with inevitable ups and downs.
The truly successful seem completely useless.
The innocent are thought guilty.
The rich plead poverty.
The perfect are thought defective.
The honest are thought corrupt.

Life is a great space with no corners —
you are always already free.
Great talent ripens late.
The greatest eloquence appears in a glance.
The greatest shape is dynamic.

The Way seems obscure and remote,
but it begins in your deepest heart.
Its benefits are given with subtlety.

41

The Way is only attractive to those who are already wise enough to know how foolish they are. Sarcastic laughter from other fools who believe themselves wise does not deter the truly wise from following the Way. Following the Way, they do not become complicated, extraordinary, and prominent. Rather, they become simple, ordinary, and subtle. They recognize cycles of change and do not lament the unstoppable rises and falls.

When fools spread lies about them, the wise state the truth but remain unperturbed when no one believes them at first. Initial failure never prevents them from trying again later. "Great talent ripens late."

42

The Way gave birth to One.
One counted self and not-self,
and gave birth to Two.
Two added duality,
and gave birth to Three.
Three played together
— beginning, middle, end —
and gave birth to numberless entities.

Energy rises to the head,
and descends to the belly.
The feeling of being arises in the heart.
Integrate the two processes,
and realize immortal harmony.

People fear abandonment,
homelessness,
bitter misfortune.
Wise leaders empathize,
and temper their rule.
Misfortune is sometimes beneficial,
and benefits are sometimes unfortunate.
The wise have always said:
"Violent men come to violent ends."
Whoever says this is my beloved teacher.

42

Energy rises to the head and descends to the belly in the current of life. The feeling of being arises in the heart to sway the head. Discipline your heart by pure love, and you light up.

43

The softest can overcome the hardest.
What requires no space transcends all space.
I recognize the advantages of non-action.
Few people ever do.

43

"What requires no space transcends all space." This is true in the most essential or absolute sense, because what "requires no space" is simultaneously everywhere and nowhere. If less can be more, then nothing can be everything.

Even in the miniaturization of technology, we see that the smaller the space required (e.g., microchips, genetic engineering, nanotechnology) the more profoundly powerful the effects.

The human adventure over many thousands of generations has involved expansion of knowledge at all size scales. We want to know everything from smallest to biggest, from sub-atomic particles to clusters of galaxies, from the origin of the universe to the end of time. The more we know, the more insight we have, the more we can do.

But doing isn't everything. We also need the balance of non-action. Whether your non-action comes only during minutes of dreamless sleep, or during periods of Zen meditation, you need it. You cannot live by action alone.

44

Which is more important,
your fame or your life?
Which is more precious,
your life or your possessions?
Which costs more: fame, riches, or loss of life?

If you have many attachments,
you are not free.
If your happiness depends on possessions,
you will be devastated by their loss.
Recognize when enough is enough,
and save yourself from troubles.
Know when to stop,
and avoid a perilous plunge.
Live long and prosper.

44

Recognize real value. Possess, but do not be possessed. Lean away from excess. Lose losing habits. To have it all, empty yourself to make room.

45

Something of great refinement appears flawed,
but is still highly useful.
Something as full as infinite space appears void,
but contains endless worlds.
Something as wonderful as life seems unfinished.
Somehow the shortest distance to your destiny
seems long and round about.
The highest technique is invisible.
Points made in silence.

Simple life uses energy to transform matter.
Human life uses mind to control energy.
Live in understanding and equanimity.
Evolve consciously.
Love gracefully.

45

The highest understanding is too subtle to say—wisdom without words. Nevertheless, transmission occurs.

We grow civilization by turning mind into matter. We grow ourselves by assuming the gratitude attitude.

46

When public and private life harmonize in the Way,
then instruments make music, not war.
When public discord and private degeneration
reinforce one another,
flat nothing results.
The worst fate of nations and individuals
is greedy discontent amidst plenty.
How can you ever let yourself be happy,
if even overabundance is not enough?
Essential happiness arises within.

46

Here is the secret of enjoying wealth without becoming corrupted by it: Own possessions, be as wealthy as you want, but don't be owned by any of it. To resist becoming possessed by your possessions, always give away a portion of your wealth. Keep up this reciprocal process, and happiness becomes your natural state.

47

Stay home,
and information streams in from the universe.
Without opening your eyes,
direct attention to the universe
in the center of your head.
Gather the facts of experience now,
and worry interpretations later.
Be wise:
Know without going.
See without looking.
Act without doing.

47

All modern communications media—from burgeoning TV to rivers of print and broadband computer floods—inundate our homes and offices with information that would have stunned someone from five generations ago. But information is not always knowledge, and knowledge is not always wisdom. Wisdom connects heart and head.

Mystical experience is usually associated with phenomena in the head. Yogis identify the structures in the center of the head with perceptions of internal lights, sounds, and images of other realms. As science unlocks the secrets of the brain, brain areas involved with mystical experiences will be discovered. Indeed, scientists have already found light sensitive cells on the pineal gland at the brain core. And this is only the beginning. What the science of the future will reveal is to become the basis for mass producing the subtle technologies of inner experience. This is good and necessary for human well-being, but not sufficient for the highest wisdom. Just as knowledge is not wisdom, neither is mere experience, no matter how grand or cosmic.

Wisdom arises from a still more fundamental component of our subtle anatomy than the brain core. As the wisest of sages have always realized, the root of essential being is in the heart, especially in the heart-beat mechanism. From here, the radiance of essential being spirals upward to illuminate the head. This mechanism lies beyond any technology. You already inhabit it, to a greater or lesser degree. It is the always present armature of reality, the structure of your essential being right now. And through deep feelings (rather than superficial emotions) you can connect with it immediately.

Live this realization and natural clarity returns. Communicate this and you illuminate the world.

When wisdom finally comes to mass media knowledge, and people accept it freely, then the world is changed. When the world is changed, then everyone can know without going, see without looking, and act without doing. The ultimate act that enlightens involves no action at all.

48

A mountain of learning grows up bit by bit.
The Way flows down in turbulence,
wearing away preconceived notions.
To live in the chaos of the moment,
simplify!
Then simplify again.
At last,
lifting a finger can move the world.
Smile with folded hands.

48

Chuang Tzu said, "Knowledge is unlimited. Life is limited. Why pursue what is unlimited with what is limited?" Accumulate knowledge, but recognize that knowledge cannot make you wise.

Mere everyday experience at the modern pace is a torrent of sensory impressions, frequent decisions, and continual doing; we cannot absorb it all, and sometimes cannot even keep pace. We must make room for stop time.

To begin to see the hidden mechanisms of the world, stop looking for them. Be still and observe yourself. Without thinking, just let it come. And go. Maintain this disposition from moment to moment during available minutes each day, and eventually under all circumstances. Then the hidden mechanisms of the world become your fingers and toes and very thoughts. "Smile with folded hands."

49

Successful people hold no fixed ideas.
Their principles are high,
but their minds are open.
They meet kindness with kindness.
They also meet hostility with kindness,
because kindness is the gesture of life.
They are faithful to the faithful.
They are also faithful to the unfaithful,
because faith is the sign of eternal life.

High speed living saturates the senses,
but successful people keep their goals in mind.
Most people gorge on sensory experiences.
Successful people attract others to their joyful state.

49

A policy of kindness shows tolerance. A policy of faithfulness opens you to the blessings of eternal life. Kindness and faith are rewarded in kind by the unlimited ultimate Source. What success could be higher?

50

Your life story began at birth.
Every human life begins the same:
three tenths vital survival strength,
three tenths body or brain debilities,
three tenths potential meant for survival
but usually squandered in a shorter life,
and one tenth mysterious essence.

Tend to your life and your story will be long.
Realize your essence,
and you'll witness the end without ending.

50

We are composite beings: $\frac{3}{10}$ vital bodily functions; $\frac{3}{10}$ individual deviations from perfect health (disabilities that may be mild or severe, whether genetic, accidental, or self-induced); $\frac{3}{10}$ learning and acculturation (which may be high or low, positive or negative); and $\frac{1}{10}$ mysterious essence, the real "you."

Do what you can to improve your life in all areas. But recognize that only cultivating your essence brings more than passing value—it brings immortality.

51

The Way connects all living beings to their Source.
Evolution nurtures them.
Competition for survival tests them.
Nature brings them to maturity.
All beings below human,
and all beings above,
are like us on the Way.
Each being is tested.
Everywhere the wise revere the Way,
and honor evolution toward spiritual success.
The Way deserves honor,
but doesn't demand it.
Success deserves honor,
but is not diminished without it.

The Way is the essence of all beings,
the current of life,
the nurse of evolution,
the space of the universe,
the home of all,
the feeder of all,
the embracer of all.

The Way does all this without possessiveness,
expectation of gratitude,
or desire for tyrannical power.
This is called absolute universal success.

51

Absolute universal success is peerless. Because it is absolute, it is unique. Because it is universal, all beings may participate in its blessing power. Because it is successful, it is utterly faithful—unhindered by doubts, possessiveness, power-lust, or unreal expectations. To be one with it, be like it.

52

The beginning of all creation
originates in the same Source.
The Source is the Mother of all.
Know the Mother,
and you may know her offspring.
Know the offspring without forgetting the Mother,
and you'll live beyond this life.

Here's how:
Spend time without stimulating
eyes, ears, nose, tongue, or touch.
Let thoughts pass without lingering.
Then life will carry you,
and to the end of your days
you will not wear out.

If you use the senses relentlessly,
think and act constantly,
then to the end of your days
there will be no remedy for your distress.

Be wise:
Observe your internal conscious process
and you will truly see.
Be flexible to be truly strong.
Use the outer, but return to the inner.
Then no harm can touch you.

52

To get some idea of the limitedness of life, consider lifespan in terms of heartbeats, or perhaps of thoughts. How many cycles can your heart and brain last if you live a typical lifespan? A large number, to be sure, but a finite one. During about ⅓ of your life you sleep. For most of the remaining ⅔, you only seem to be awake. In reality, much of your so-called "waking life" is lived on automatic. The moments when you are in touch with your essence are few and far between. But you can remember every one of them if you permit yourself.

Every such moment is a message from the mystery at the core of your being. Consider each one carefully. Meditate on them. Eventually and inevitably, understanding appears.

Meditation is nothing special. It's just the other side of active life. Balance action with periods of non-action. Alternately employ reality and contemplate it. "Use the outer, but return to the inner. Then no harm can touch you."

53

If I was the least bit intelligent,
I'd live in accord with the Way,
and my only fear would be straying.
The Way is really smooth and straight,
but people are always devising useless shortcuts.

If government thrives while the land is abused,
and people starve;
If the social elite wear expensive clothes,
and spend fortunes on their appearance;
If weapons pervade society at every level;
If entertainment and parties are the highest goal;
If every excess is still not enough;
This is robbery disguised as civilization.
This is not the Way.

53

In every age of unjust government, cultural frivolity, social turmoil, and wars, a few angry figures have cried out with apocalyptic warnings. Some warnings were indeed prophetic, while others turned out to be utterly wrong. But at the moment they were uttered, no one knew for certain if any prediction would come to pass.

So it is today. Post-modern dreads make up the daily news. Pick your disaster ... you know them all. But in generations to come, when our great grandchildren are helping their children learn history, which of our dreads will seem truly dreadful, and which merely silly?

This is not the end of the world. There is suffering, as there has always been, but there is real improvement, too. Slowly but surely, one person at a time, humanity is evolving. Amid all the horrors of this "robbery disguised as civilization," there are yet living jewels of love in many human hearts.

Someday those hearts will soar. And that day is not far off.

54

Whatever has deep historical roots can't be uprooted.
Whatever is deeply embraced can't slip away.
Those who have succeeded in realizing their essence
have been honored for generations after.

Realize your essence,
and your character becomes genuine.
Bring your understanding to kinship,
and your family thrives.
Bring your understanding to public affairs,
and your country flourishes.
Bring your understanding to the universe,
and your influence is all-pervasive.

To know another,
know yourself.
To know other families,
know your own.
To know other countries,
know your own.

How do I know this?
By knowing myself.

54

    Realize your essence and you grow in true character. Your family thrives. Thriving families are the foundation of a flourishing country. Flourishing countries help neighboring countries by free trade. Thriving relations lead to international peace.

    Where does universal peace begin? Inside you.

55

Real success is like being a newborn baby.
No insects, birds, or animals devour it.
Its bones are tender,
muscles soft,
but feel its grip!
No one told it about sex,
but its sex organs already know the story.
Why?
Integral vitality.
It can howl all day without tiring.
Why?
Integral harmony.

To experience harmony is to know success.
To recognize what works successfully in the world
is to have insight.
This is the Way.

To avoid all risks
is to invite disaster.
To pursue mental fantasies
drains energy from intelligence.
To force growth
is to accelerate decay.
None of this is in accord with the Way.
Whatever is not in accord with the Way
will not last.

55

What is more precious than a child? Baby means new life. New life means new hope. Hope is harmonious, happy, and whole, like a natural child. Like a child, hope must take risks in order to grow, because "to avoid all risks is to invite disaster."

Growing means learning. Learn not to confuse mental fantasies with real hope, and forced growth with harmonious development. What is false and forced is contrary to the Way, and so cannot long endure. What is true and free lasts forever. Be true and free.

56

The one who knows doesn't speak.
The one who speaks doesn't know.

In solitude from the senses,
witless and relaxed,
awareness turned inward,
obstructions to flow removed —
oneness with the subtle Source.

The paradox is this:
You can't get closer to it by wishing,
and you couldn't run away from it if you tried.
You can't help it,
and you can't harm it.
Yet you can realize essential Oneness.
This is the ultimate truth of all universes.

56

Ultimate truth is paradoxical; it unites opposites. The ultimate truth of your condition is always already perfect. But it can take a lifetime (or many lifetimes) to realize this. It's like going home, yet knowing it truly for the first time.

Vast numbers of people are "going home" in our common Positive Futures.

57

In government, serve honestly.
In war, use surprise.
To win the world, don't meddle.
Why?
Because the more rules and taboos,
the more difficulties for people.
The more weapons proliferate,
the poorer people become,
and the more danger disorders the world.
The more devious and dishonest people become,
the more strange things happen.
The more laws written,
the more dissidents and criminals.

The greatest leaders have always said:
"I let people work things out for themselves.
I have peace of mind,
and they adapt to reality.
I permit enterprise,
and they grow rich.
I control my own desires,
and they simply get things done."

57

"To win the world," Lao Tzu says, we should minimize rules, taboos, weapons, laws, deviousness, and dishonesty.

How can this be done?

Not by making rules against rules. Not by using guns and force. Not by laws. Nor by devious trickery. Those are not the tools of a great leader. Anyone employing them hurries toward disaster.

Benign non-interference brings spontaneous order. Leaders and followers of that order, Lao Tzu says, "let people work things out for themselves."

58

When government is made of liberties,
the people are simply happy.
When government is made of controls,
the people lie unhappily.
After disaster comes rescue.
After long contentment, distress.
Who knows how things will ultimately turn out?
What used to work is no longer appropriate.
What was once good turns evil.
People have long been perplexed
by unpredictable turnabouts in life.

One who is truly successful
smooths out the cycle.
One who is truly successful
turns up and downs into forward motion.
One who is truly successful
is sharp but not prickly.
One who is truly successful
doesn't build himself up by tearing others down.
One who is truly successful
shines without glaring.

58

True success is not measured in money—it is measured in accomplishments. Great accomplishments range from the completion of monumental projects, to simply taking failure with grace and good humor.

Ups and downs are inevitable in life. The only thing you can really control is your reaction to them.

Learn from failure, and you will eventually achieve success. Be tough-minded and kind-hearted. "Shine without glaring."

59

In government and in following the Way,
the best policy is to avoid
unnecessary activities and expenses.
Living things are naturally
thrifty with matter and energy.
To be natural is to be thrifty.
To realize the essence of life
is to succeed against any difficulty.
After succeeding against difficulties,
you can break through limitations.
Without limits, you realize who you truly are.
Your success began with your first step on the Way.
The Way can lead you to serve in leadership.
Then you can share your blessings for generations.

59

By paring away the unnecessary, you discard dragging limitations. "Without limits, you realize who you truly are." Then you find your feet on the Way. You gradually discover that you can help others in this life and beyond, sharing your blessings "for generations."

60

Governing a large country is like raising small fish:
the more you agitate them,
the worse off they are.
When you apply the Way in daily life,
all your bodily and mental parts integrate.
You become capable of wonders.
But you refrain from harm,
and casual miracles.
When you apply the Way to government,
all sides are heard from,
and the statecraft of liberty emerges.

When contemplation of the Way becomes unity,
your body relaxes,
and your mind expands in wonder.
Paradoxical consciousness—
not separate from anything,
yet still animating one body.
Paradoxical destiny—
accomplishing wonders,
yet needing nothing more than you already are.

60

In government, liberty. In daily life, integrity. In contemplation, oneness. By these three, balance life for the good of one and all. Balance the world in Positive Futures.

61

A great country attracts small ones,
like rivers flowing to the sea.
The sea is the mother of the world.
The feminine wins over the masculine
through gentle submission.
She lies low, yet mounts high.
So if a great country lowers itself
before a small one,
it wins friendship and trust.
If a small country lowers itself
before a great one,
it wins friendship and support.
One wins by taking the lower position,
the other wins by remaining low.
To maintain peaceful balance,
the great must be humble.

61

When the great are humble, they win friendship and trust. The feminine conquers through gentle submission to the masculine. This has been nature's way for countless generations.

Men and women are equal but unique. The strategies built into their genes, and the social structures that have evolved from those strategies, are necessarily different. But they have this in common: Mutual loving submission in marriage is the key to sexual satisfaction, emotional security, and lifelong friendship. Each man and each woman must find this out by trying it out. For hints on how it's done, look to tradition.

62

The Way is the essential foundation of all.
The wise treasure it,
yet even scoundrels and fools
can take refuge in it.
Fine words will find buyers.
Fine services will find takers.
Though deluded people may lose the Way,
the Way never loses them.

When appointing leaders,
instead of filling the moment
with the expensive grandeur of office,
simply indicate the Way.

Why do the wise esteem the Way?
Because they say,
"Seek and you shall find;
correct your errors and you will know truth."
That is why the Way is the free treasure that protects itself.

62

Never despair that you have lost the Way. Separation is delusion. Indeed, the delusion of separation is the root error. You don't need to do anything in particular to be on the Way. Look for it and you will find "the free treasure that protects itself."

63

Act without moving a muscle.
Remake yourself without lifting a finger.
Taste the new flavor of your stress-free body chemistry.
Regard the heights and depths of worldly life with equanimity.
Respond to all with a policy of kindness.

If you want real success,
get beyond wanting.
Assign no value to mountains of money.
Learn what isn't taught in school.
Induce people to recognize the essential treasure
they have overlooked.

63

How can you act without moving a muscle? Change your mind. How can you remake yourself without lifting a finger? Change your heart. Equanimity and kindness will blossom.

If you want something strongly enough, you'll have it. If you want to stop wanting strongly enough, you'll have that, too. The essential treasure is always within your grasp.

64

Address difficulties when they are easy.
Build great accomplishments from small beginnings.
Prepare for rough spots while the going is still smooth.
Control things before they peak in force.
Deal with danger before it appears.
Manage simple hardness with easy softness.
Defuse hateful anger before violent explosion.
All this is called "nipping it in the bud."

The tallest tree grew from a tiny sprout.
The tallest building began with one scoop of dirt.
The longest journey begins with a single step.
Successful people aim for high goals
by starting to work at the bottom
right now.
That's why they succeed.

Casual promises don't inspire much confidence.
If you begin a project with a cynical joke,
the laugh will be on you.
If you are prepared for hardship,
it will never defeat you.
Many people give up
when they are just about to succeed.
Pay close attention at the beginning,
persevere patiently to the end,
and nothing will come to ruin.

64

Your own Positive Futures begin in this moment. All you have is right now. Every goal is possible from here. But even if you're on the right track, you'll get run over if you just sit there. Take the first step.

Whatever you undertake, do it with full intent to succeed. Cynicism fails itself. Stick to your path, facing difficulties with positive humor. Concentrate, proceed, and succeed.

65

Throughout the ages,
the most wise practitioners of the Way
have not encouraged uninformed debate.
Instead, they have discarded preconceived ideas
so they could observe as pure witnesses.
Why does government arise,
yet people are still unruly?
Because the lives of people have become too complicated.
Some leaders try outsmarting the people
by thinking up ever more complicated schemes,
but end up bringing on calamities.
Wise leaders take things simply,
constructing solutions of bare elegance,
and delivering real benefits.

Be wise:
Recognize the power of observation
and the strength of simplicity.
Measure what you observe and what you do.
Simplify for sure success.
This principle applies on many levels.
It leads ultimately against entropic decay
and home to the original One.

65

The perfect government is uncomplicated and unobtrusive, with few burdens and prudent benefits. The perfect solution is simple and direct, without layers of devious, bureaucratic complications.

Forget your preconceptions and observe what's really going on. Look at our world as if you've just come from another planet. See how strange things are. Study them until you understand. Then you'll succeed in your new home. Succeed here and you'll understand how to return to your real, original Home.

66

How did the ocean become queen
of all rivers and streams?
Because it is lower than they are.

Likewise, if you have humility,
you can serve everyone.
By putting yourself last,
the people will acclaim you their leader.
When you lead with this wisdom,
the burdens of the people are light.
In appearances before the people,
they see you clearly.
So they follow wherever you lead,
and never tire of your presence.

66

A faithful servant is humble, and so is fit for leadership. Faithful servants take the lower position, supporting all above them. Forget about abstractions like "the people," in whose name so many have needlessly suffered and died. A good servant serves one person at a time, until all have been served. When people see such service, they acclaim the servant their leader.

67

Many people listen to the Way I describe and say:
"Sounds great, but strange."
Because it is not conventional wisdom,
the Way maintains it greatness.

I embrace whole-heartedly three treasures:
Kindness;
Simplicity;
Not always trying to be "Number One."

Be kind,
and you will have the courage to serve others.
Be simple,
and you will develop greatness.
Do not try to be "Number One" all the time,
and events will proceed naturally.
Then you can grow without distress.

If you try to be brave without being kind—
If you have great plans without a simple life—
If you take power without self-sacrifice—
then you are heading for disaster.

Kindness after war can win peace.
Kindness against hostility can win security.
Kindness attracts kindness,
from other people and the universe,
giving you protective support.

67

"Kindness attracts kindness." Do to the universe as you would have the universe do to you.

68

Successful warriors control their violence.
Successful fighters don't rush offensives.
The best victory comes by allowing the enemy
to fall of his own weight.
The best commander has humility,
and is not contentious.
This unites the efforts of others.
Follow this, and you follow the subtle law.

68

Successful combatants have self-control, forcing the enemy "to fall of his own weight" as in the martial art of Aikido. The enemy attacks, and thereby moves out of balance. The defender needs minimal effort to defeat an unbalanced foe. A warrior blends with life.

Successful commanders use humility to unite individuals in coordinated effort. Humility means openness to cooperation without self-importance. Successful commanders unite individuals in cooperative efforts by listening to even the humblest among them. Everyone who leads, or follows, in this manner, is truly following the subtle law.

69

The strategists say this:
"Dare not to host a battle,
but be an uninvited guest.
If you dare not attack,
then only defend.
Dare not to advance one bit,
but draw out the enemy
by retreating even more.

"Advance where obstacles have been removed.
Grasp the advantage where no confrontation can happen.
Attack the undefended points.
Hide your weapons.

"The biggest mistake is to underestimate an opponent.
This can be fatal.
So in the battle of opposing forces,
the side that does not glorify war wins it."

69

Protect home and country before the enemy can reach you. Use offense or defense, as the situation requires. Lure the enemy to your advantage. When a clear path of opportunity opens, move quickly. Bypass enemy strong points, attacking weak ones all the while. Conceal your forces. And never, ever underestimate an opponent. Fight for right, not glory, and your cause will prevail.

70

My words are very easy to understand.
They are very easy to practice.
Yet many people don't understand them
or practice them.
My words come from a single source.
My actions are caused by a single master.
Most people have no knowledge of this.
That's why they have no knowledge of me.
The fewer who know me,
the better the ones who follow me.
So the wise person dresses plainly
and carries a treasure within.

70

We are composite creatures, dwelling in a realm of sensation and spirit somewhere between apes and angels. Our many parts, if unintegrated, tend to pull us apart. Lao Tzu speaks from the singular perspective of integrity when he says "My words come from a single source. My actions are caused by a single master."

How to act from a single source, to have a single master? Begin by observing yourself.

71

If you regard your knowledge as tentative,
you have insight.
If you doubt the possibility of true knowledge,
you are deeply sick.
Only when you are sick of this sickness
can your nihilism be cured.
If you turn your mind to simple understanding
you will not be sick,
because you will not mistake concepts for truth.
This is the secret of mental health.

71

Pay attention and you'll understand. Doubt the mere possibility of ever understanding, and you'll go mad. Understanding comes after intense observation. Doubt comes after discouragement. Persevere in observation, and understanding arises naturally. Become discouraged and doubtful, and you prevent your own understanding.

Knowledge may come quickly or slowly. If it comes quickly, make good use of it. If it comes slowly, then you must act without sufficient knowledge. So be kind. You may not always know what is true, but you will always know what is kind.

72

When people lose their sense of wonder,
it is no wonder they lose their good sense.
The mere fact of existence is the greatest wonder.
So treat your home with respect,
no matter how lowly it might be.
Treat your life and work with respect,
no matter how lowly they might be.
Because you respect your life and work,
you will never tire of life.

Successful people know themselves,
but they are not egotists.
Successful people love themselves,
but they are not pretentious.
Successful people look at the world with wonder,
and respect.
This is why successful people keep
what is right for them,
and give away the rest.

72

Consider the miracle of existence. Such a wonder is awe-inspiring. Respect for it all, and for your part in it, makes life worth living. Love and be loved, have and give, and you will never be found wanting.

73

If you think bravery is the same as recklessness,
your end will come unnaturally soon.
If you think bravery is deliberate action,
you will be preserved.
Recklessness is harmful.
Deliberation benefits liberally.
Through subtle influences
the invisible forces of the universe
ruin the reckless,
yet most people don't know why.
So even the wise,
already integrated with the Way,
don't take the universe for granted.
They know the universe responds
to their actions and their thoughts.
They know if they lose their humor,
the universe plays a deadly joke on them.
The subtle law of response is the key to the universe.
You become like what you concentrate upon.

The subtle Origin of this universe and all universes
informs many orders of harmonious space and time.
The most fundamental order is the subtle law.
It responds with exquisite sensitivity
to every movement
of every being
in every moment
in every universe,
yet never says a word.

You didn't call it, but it comes to you.
You didn't plan it, but its plan is perfect.
The wise have always known this:
"The vast subtle energy net of the universe
has huge spaces between its strands,
yet nothing slips through it!"

73

Your destiny is in your own hands. Regardless of what may befall you in this life due to the actions of others or simple accident, the way you respond to life is the crucial, deciding factor. If your response is positive, compassionate, and wise, you will realize your destiny. If your response is negative, self-obsessed, and foolish, you will merely experience your fate.

Fate is what happens to you if and when you abandon all hope of a higher destiny. Then fate takes over. It appears in the form of a disordered life wherein nothing makes sense. You seem to be ruled by a series of accidents, each one propelling you into a new dead end wall. Then you bounce off, only to find yourself heading for another wall. Fate is life as a racquet ball.

Destiny is life as an actor. You take deliberate actions, moving forward toward your goal. Nothing can stop you for long. Every time an obstacle blocks your path, you find a way around it. Every accident that slows—or even reverses—your progress for a while is just another test of your adaptability. Perseverance always succeeds. Even if you die while persevering toward a goal in life, you do not perish. You still advance toward your real goal, your destiny. And death is not the end of your story. Many possible Positive Futures await you.

74

If people face death as fearless martyrs,
why bother threatening them with death?
On the other hand,
if people cling to their lives,
and outlaws are surely caught and executed,
who would dare commit crime?

But if you take hateful charge of the killing,
the subtle law returns it to you.
If you become an executioner
taking personal vengeance
in the name of the law,
you're like a toddler
with a lethal weapon:
You will not escape unscathed.

74

Martyrs, or prisoners of conscience, can often have a larger effect on human affairs after death than they had in life. There is neither justice nor political sense in executing them.

On the other hand, criminals should be punished, because if "outlaws are surely caught and executed, who would dare commit crime?"

One of the legitimate functions of government, or conflict resolution organizations, is to provide equal justice and fit punishment for individuals regardless of their status in society, and without the ugliness of personal vengeance, which always returns to harm the avenger. Paupers and presidents can both be called to justice by the courts, but should never be judged and punished by mob violence.

Just punishment, including the death penalty, must fit the crime, so long as this act is in accord with the common sense of the greater mass of individuals in society. To do otherwise would be neither fair nor compassionate. Mercy to the guilty is cruelty to the innocent.

75

Why do people live in poverty and strife?
Because their rulers get fat on taxes.
That's why people live in poverty and strife.

Why are people difficult to manage?
Because meddling by their rulers causes distress.
That's why people are difficult to manage.

Why do people joke about death and taxes?
Because their rulers take too much for themselves,
and care only for personal power and prestige.
That's why people joke about death and taxes.

Live for more than yourself,
and you'll know the value of every life.

75

"Why do people live in poverty and strife?...taxes." If you, as a government official, tax something, you discourage it. Tax wealth, and you will ultimately get more general poverty. Poverty does not grow in spite of government programs to end it, but because of them. Subsidize something and you get more of it; tax something and you get less. Such a pernicious taxing and spending policy is the worst of both worlds.

Low taxes help to create more wealth. Encourage business—the enterprise of free people—and everyone benefits. Freedom to think and to do according to your own conscience is the key. Alternately compete and cooperate with others in this game called life. The point of the game is to "Live for more than yourself, and you'll know the value of every life."

76

During life,
you are soft and supple.
At death,
you become hard and rigid.
When a plant is alive,
it is pliant and tender.
When a plant is dead,
it is dry and brittle.
So the hard and rigid
are the companions of death.
The soft and supple
are the companions of life.

That's why an army ruled by an iron fist
is ripe for defeat.
A dry tree is ready for the ax.
The proud and mighty will begin to collapse.
The soft and gentle sprout will rise above them all!

76

Be adaptable and humble, lively but not proud, and the flowers of your life can bloom amid concrete.

77

The subtle law of the universe
stretches like a bow.
It bends down the top.
It lifts up the bottom.
Pull back the string,
and it is tensed outside
and compressed inside
while the arrow sits calmly.
Release the string,
and it relaxes its energy
by propelling the arrow with a snap.
It's the nature of the subtle law
to take energy from the energetic
and give it to the inert.

Human beings seldom follow this law.
Rulers take from both poor and rich.
They give promises to the poor
while enriching themselves
and their favorites
in the name of the people.
Only the wise of the Way
always have something to give.
So the wise give,
but don't cling;
They accomplish many tasks,
but don't linger over their accomplishments.
They don't want to be envied,
or considered superior.

77

Lao Tzu advocated kind but limited government. Government is a fine balance between helping, and hurting, people with different interests.

Give the people as much autonomy as possible, and let them work out their own relations in good faith. Too much government is an affront to the competence of people to live in liberty. Governments that meddle, muddle.

78

Water is soft and yielding.
Yet there's nothing like water
for wearing down the hardest things.
No one can deny this!
Yielding overcomes the strong.
Softness overcomes the hard.
Many people know this,
but few understand how to practice it.

The wise have always known:
"If you can stand to suffer indignities for your countrymen,
you are qualified to lead them.
If you can suffer calamities for your country,
you are qualified to run the state.
Its seems paradoxical—
by taking the heat you become great!"

78

The reason governments exist is the same reason tribes exist—human beings, like other primates, naturally follow leaders. This is true in all levels of social relations, whether in families, tribes, or nations. Since we are genetically bound by this tendency to need leaders, we should pick good ones. Lao Tzu tells us what to look for: "If you can stand to suffer indignities for your countrymen, you are qualified to lead them."

79

Even after disputes are settled by agreement or treaty,
some resentment is likely to remain.
Do you call this satisfactory?

Someone must risk returning injury with kindness,
or hostility will never turn to goodwill.
So the wise always give without expecting gratitude.

Wise people recognize their debts to the world.
Wise people repay the world by serving others.
Fools treat the world like debt collectors.
They demand snappy service.
Although the subtle law of the universe
doesn't play favorites,
it supports the wise unfailingly.

79

The wise succeed because they recognize the subtle law of the universe. They give to receive, and receive with gratitude. They are slow to anger, quick to forgive. Although they do not consider themselves special, they are upheld unfailingly by the Most High.

80

Imagine a small land with few inhabitants.
They own ships of all kinds,
yet they never move to foreign lands.
The inhabitants love life in their land so dearly,
no one wants to move to another place.
They own every kind of vehicle,
but they never bother to travel in them.
They have very powerful weapons,
but they never resort to using them.
They write a few notes to order their simple affairs,
living like sophisticated primitives.
They are content with healthy food,
pleased with useful clothing,
satisfied in snug homes,
and protective of their way of life.
The country next door is in shouting distance,
but people during their whole lives
rarely leave their homeland.

80

The simple but happy land that Lao Tzu describes is the goal of many hearts. Some wish to build it. Others seek to find it. In fact, attainment of this land has already been accomplished by some. This happy place is located at the second-highest level of the realm we all experience after death. Between Earth and the highest Heaven, this paradise exists as the penultimate place. It sits just outside the threshold of Heaven, the Domain of God. As on Earth, life and death exist in this second-highest paradise, too. But when a person dies to that place, the next stop is the everlasting home, the Domain of God.

Many names have been given to this blessed land on the outskirts of Heaven. Some Jews and Christians call it the Sixth of the Seven Heavens. Some Muslims call it the Paradise of the Elect. Some Buddhists call it the Western Paradise, while others call it the Tushita Heaven. Some Hindus call it the Realm of the Siddhas. As for me, I just call it the Bright Land.

The Bright Land on the outskirts of Heaven is free of poverty, scarcity, drudgery, bureaucracy, crime, sickness, and fear. Life is long and happy there. When death approaches someone in the Bright Land, that person is surrounded by loved ones and dies with a smile, secure in the knowledge that the next destination is the Domain of God.

Our destiny is the Bright Land. It is the place where all of our individual Positive Futures overlap. We can all hope for it after death. But our reason for being here is to build it on this plane. Death is not a prerequisite for receiving many of the blessings of existence in the Bright Land. Human destiny consists of approximating our own more modest, but still blessed, version of it in this universe. In the natural evolution of spirituality and science, of society and technology, we are gaining all the tools necessary to build paradise.

A purported paradise on Earth is usually called a utopia because it is considered impossible. "Utopia" literally means "no place" in Greek. Human utopias have always failed because they isolated themselves from the rest of humanity, restricted free thought and free enterprise, and refused to evolve into anything better.

Unlike any such utopia, the Bright Land that is our destiny is a land where freedom is the discipline and happiness the responsibility of each and all. And unlike the "no place" of failed utopias, the model for our Bright Land already exists on the spiritual plane. It is not "no place." The Bright Land is real. Although we cannot get there easily from here, we can all hope to get there eventually. In the meantime, we can fashion our own Bright Land in human time.

The Bright Land we will build over generations to come is beginning now, in our era. We are already creating the prerequisites, as the many cultural streams of humanity interact and learn from one another. We are witnessing the gestation of a new civilization. Revolutionary new technologies to move atoms and repair DNA will allow us to refashion our world and ourselves, while the wisdom of the ages shows us how to cultivate what is essential.

In a world refashioned to approximate the Bright Land, people live in intimate communities, where education, religion, science, art, and commerce take place on the human scale. Vast technologies will underlie this seeming simplicity, removing drudgery and creating nearly limitless material wealth. Freed from economic necessity by the new technologies, people will again value people. The new norm of value becomes human service. Living, loving, and learning freely together, we all prosper.

In our Bright Land, your life could span centuries. Or longer. You will have vast opportunities for experience, knowledge, and accomplishments. No satisfaction is beyond reach if you live long enough. In time, though, you will tire of material and sensual satisfactions. Then you will be ready for the most important thing of all. The longer you remain alert and lively—paying attention to the lesson of each moment—the greater your chances for realizing the spiritual wisdom of your essence. When you are ready, a teacher appears.

And when death finally comes in our Bright Land, you will be surrounded by loved ones and die with a smile, secure in the knowledge that your next destination will be positive: You will either leave the Bright Land in this universe and go to the Bright Land on the spiritual plane, or—better still—you may finally enter directly into the Domain of God.

To build our own version of the Bright Land, we will use spirit, science, and technology working together in free markets to become wiser, richer, healthier, and better. We will banish scarcity by making efficient use of the material and energy resources of Earth through the pollutionless micromachines of nanotechnology. In space, we will create niches for Earth-life to expand and diversify. Everywhere, we will eliminate sickness through healthy living and biotechnology, and ensure justice to cultivate peace, fair dealings, and security. Most important of all, we will apply spiritual wisdom to balance the needs of our animal nature with the needs of our essential, spiritual nature.

Our human species has evolved over many generations to what it is now. During most of those previous generations, the pace of life was slower, moving to a different rhythm. We evolved to that rhythm. To practice traditional spiritual disciplines intensively, we need to able to return to that rhythm. In the Bright Land of wealth and opportunity, where the marriage of spirituality and science has been consummated, there is time for everything at the right pace, including highly personalized forms of spiritual instruction and practice.

This evolution is our destiny. It is *not* too good to be true. It is both good and true. But building the Bright Land is not easy. It will take time. There will be setbacks. Still, what better goal to work toward? Your inheritance is the Positive Futures of paradise.

81

The truth isn't always pretty.
Pretty things aren't always true.
Goodness doesn't argue.
Arguing isn't good.
A person of deep understanding may have little education.
An educated person may have little deep understanding.

Good people are successful without being preoccupied
with amassing endless wealth.
The more they live for others,
the richer their lives become.
The more they give, the more they get.
The essential nature of the universe of universes
is benefit, not harm.
The nature of the absolute being
extends goodness unconditionally and universally,
and doesn't pick fights with anyone.

81

Look behind the surface of things. Accept the truth of the current situation. Then change the situation. Recognize the paradox that nothing needs to be added to your state, yet there are great things to be accomplished. Work, but recognize the non-necessity of everything.

To get a lot, give a lot. To get to the Bright Land, give a hand to the work crew. Take the next step on the journey to the Bright Land right now by affirming the highest possibilities you can imagine.

You already know deep inside yourself that your highest destiny is the Domain of God. This is your ultimate Positive Future. Even now in your mind's eye, you can see the threshold just ahead. A radiant figure waits to greet you. Welcome, friend!

Epilogue
The Return of No Return

Many years earlier, Lao Tzu had passed through Han Gu Pass and into the Mystery. One night the old guard, now retired and frail, sat in meditation in his mountain hut. As usual, his eyes were half-closed. The darkness inside the hut was complete, except for one small candle.

In a flash, the room was illumined by pearly white radiance. Lao Tzu appeared before the old guard, looking just as he had decades before. Overcome with joy, the old guard prostrated himself flat upon the floor in humble gratitude. "Master!" he cried.

Lao Tzu spoke softly. "You have done well. Soon you will leave that body."

The old guard slowly rose to a sitting position. He gazed at Lao Tzu without surprise. "I know. Please take me with you now! I know there are many realms after death. I beg you, Master, guide me to the right one!"

Lao Tzu smiled with infinite love. "I will be your sign. Look for me at the threshold of Light. But I am only one of many Guides for human beings. Each who dies must look for the right threshold personality. I am yours."

Lao Tzu burst out in hearty laughter. "But your time is not yet, my friend. You have an appointment to keep." The radiance of Lao Tzu departed.

Feeling extremely tired, the old guard lay down on his bed and immediately fell asleep. Soon he dreamed that he stood in a beautiful land of rolling green hills and scattered trees. And he knew he was dreaming.

To his right a spring bubbled into a tiny stream. He followed the narrow, trickling waterway to a large, calm pond, where he saw a youth sitting on a large rock, gazing into the water. The old guard hailed the young man, who ignored him. He approached the man, stood next to him, and looked into the pond.

A flash of light sparked in the middle of the water. At the center of the flash, which quickly faded, a tiny pearl of light remained. The pearl expanded rapidly. As the expansion continued, the pearl broke into tiny points of light. The tiny points of light clumped into whorls, and the whorls into clusters, and the clusters into filaments in sinuous dance.

Patterns of light continued to swirl within the circumference of expansion. Expansion slowed as the dancing lights approached the shoreline of the pond, stopped, and began to retreat. Reversing the old expansion in stages, the tiny lights gradually contracted—then suddenly coalesced into one, ending where it had begun. Darkness covered the face of the waters.

Turning his face from the water, the youth spoke to the old guard. "You have just seen one cycle of creation. You were sent there to experience part of it—to be blessed, taught, and tested." He smiled. "And you did well!"

"Soon" the youth continued, gesturing at the peaceful landscape around them, "you will join us here. Lao Tzu said to expect you."

The old guard was elated. He was about to speak, when the youth raised a finger and said, "You have one more task remaining. Look behind you!"

Turning, the old guard looked down as if from a mountain in the clouds. He fell and awoke, startled. Golden dawn light limned the sole window of the tiny hut.

From a distance came the sound of approaching footsteps, then a knock at the door. The old guard rose slowly but eagerly from his bed, and shuffled across the room, thoughts racing wildly. He felt certain that his final act on Earth would begin on the other side of that door. Hands trembling, he opened the door.

A young man, the very same one he had seen in his dream, bowed before him. But here and now the man had hollow cheeks and was dressed in rags. The youth did not seem like a maker of worlds.

"Please, reverend sir," the young man implored, "I am a poor seeker of truth. I have traveled many days to see you. Please show me the Way."

The old guard smiled kindly. "You are welcome in my humble home, sir. Please enter."

The youth entered and sat. The old man reached into a wooden box, removed a silk bundle, and unwrapped a sheaf of old papers. He gave the poems to his guest, one at a time.

The man bowed as he accepted each poem. He read each in silence. The old guard observed the man's face as he read, watching his eyebrows. First the eyebrows knotted, then relaxed as understanding came.

After the last poem had been read by his guest, the old guard spoke. "I am not long for this world. I am going to a better place. Please take this treasure given to me by Lao Tzu."

The old guard rose slowly to his feet. "Now I must say good-bye to you, sir . . . until we meet again."

The young man smiled. "Yes," he said, "I dreamed that we will meet again."

The two bowed and parted. But only for a while. Isn't that always the way?

Acknowledgements

I acknowledge with gratitude my infinite debt to the Giver of Life, in Whom I live and breathe and have my being, and of Whose Consciousness I am a modification. As are you.

I acknowledge with gratitude Lao Tzu and all of the other saints, sages, and teachers, especially Jesus Christ, Gautama Buddha, Da Avabhasa, Franklin Merrell-Wolff, Chuang Tzu, Shankara, Meister Eckhart, Elijah, Hui Neng, Yogananda, Francis of Assisi, John of the Cross, Seraphim of Sarov, Saint Patrick, Thomas Merton, Mother Teresa, Ni (Hua-Ching), Oscar Ichazo, Kwan Saihung, Ken McGuire, John Economos, Wendy Palmer, Tomas Burger, C. S. Lewis, and Robert Anton Wilson.

I acknowledge with gratitude the scientific work of all contributors in those disciplines, especially Albert Einstein, Werner Heisenberg, Stephen Hawking, Roger Penrose, John Wheeler, Richard Feynman, Freeman Dyson, Lee Smolin, Robert Jastrow, Arthur C. Clarke, Isaac Asimov, Gerard O'Neill, Fred Alan Wolf, Fritjof Capra, James Lovelock, John Lilly, Adam Smith, F. A. Hayek, Edward O. Wilson, Richard Dawkins, Christopher G. Langton, Stuart A. Kauffman, Norman Packard, K. Eric Drexler, H. Keith Henson, and Mike Darwin.

I acknowledge with gratitude those who helped make this book possible, especially my publisher and friend, Richard Grossinger, book designer Paula Morrison and typesetter Catherine Campaigne.

I acknowledge with gratitude and love what I have received from my entire family, especially from my parents Michael N. and Frances LaTorra, my wife Grace, and my son Sage, as well as my in-laws Thomas and Patricia Puckett. Thanks for many yesterdays—and for every today.

I acknowledge with gratitude the Visitor.